GET BY IN
HINDI&URDU

D0550997

**A quick beginners' course for those
working with Hindi and Urdu
speakers in Britain,
with a section for travellers
to India and Pakistan.**

Course writer
Dr Alison Shaw

Producer
Kathy Flower

BBC Books

Get by in Hindi & Urdu
A BBC Radio Course
First broadcast in Autumn 1989

Published to accompany a series of programmes prepared in
consultation with the Continuing Education Advisory Council

Illustrations by Claire Nias

Published by BBC Books, a division of BBC Enterprises Limited,
Woodlands, 80 Wood Lane, London W12 0TT

ISBN 0 563 21485 6
First published 1989
Reprinted 1990
© The author and the British Broadcasting Corporation 1989

Set in 10 on 11 point Univers Medium

Printed and bound in Great Britain by
Martin's of Berwick Limited

Cover printed by Richard Clay Ltd, Norwich

Contents

4 chaar

About Hindi and Urdu

Hindi is the national language of India and Urdu is the national language of Pakistan. In their everyday spoken forms, Hindi and Urdu are almost identical, though they are written in different scripts.

Hindi Script: चाय

pronounced: *chaae*
meaning 'tea'

Urdu script: چاۓ

The everyday spoken form of Hindi/Urdu is called Hindi by non-Muslims and Urdu by Muslims. At this everyday spoken level, there are a few differences according to whether the speaker is Muslim or Hindu: for example the greetings differ, and the days of the week have different names. Where there are differences, both versions are given in this course.

Who speaks Hindi and Urdu

Across northern and central India and in Pakistan perhaps 200 million people speak Hindi and Urdu. For some, it is a mother-tongue; for others it is a 'link language' spoken in addition to a regional language. It is also the language used in the highly popular films; India produces about 800 films a year, and millions of Indians and Pakistanis go regularly whatever their mother tongue. In Britain, Hindi/Urdu is the first or second language of Indian and Pakistani settlers, and is used in radio and television programmes for south Asian audiences.

Other Indian languages

In India and Pakistan there are many other regional languages besides Hindi and Urdu. Most Pakistani settlers in Britain, being from the Punjab district, have Punjabi as their mother-tongue, while most Indians in Britain, being from the Punjab or from Gujarat, speak Punjabi or Gujarati, languages which are related to Hindi/Urdu. But they use Hindi/Urdu as a 'link language', often borrowing English words.

Why learn Hindi/Urdu

This course is mainly for people such as health workers, social workers and teachers who want to be able to talk to Indians and Pakistanis settled in Britian who don't speak English fluently. By learning Hindi/Urdu a tutor of English can discover why particular features of English are difficult for Hindi/Urdu speakers to get right. A health worker may find that by using her own faltering Hindi/Urdu she actually encourages a Pakistani woman who seems to know no English to speak in English! Even a limited knowledge of Hindi/Urdu can be a great ice-breaker.

Hindi/Urdu is now probably the most commonly spoken language in Britain after English, spoken and understood by the approximately 760,000 Indians and 397,000 Pakistanis settled in Britain (*Social Trends*, 1989). You don't need to go abroad to enjoy the pleasures of using another language, for there are many opportunities for socialising with Indians and Pakistanis in shops and restaurants, at work and at home. Even if your Hindi/Urdu is incorrect, or you don't get beyond being able to greet someone appropriately and ask how they are, Hindi/Urdu speakers will be delighted that you have made the effort. This will apply even if you speak to a Bangladeshi whose mother-tongue is Sylheti!

If you are planning a trip to India or Pakistan, Hindi/Urdu will be useful in Pakistan and right across northern India, even, to some extent, in Nepal. It will still be useful, though to a lesser extent, in southern India or Sri Lanka. The languages spoken there, of which the major one is Tamil, are of a different, Dravidian, origin. Of course, many educated Indians and Pakistanis speak English, so you can always get by with that.

About this course

The aim of this course is to help you to speak and understand simple everyday phrases, so you won't find the Hindi or Urdu script used. We have used letters of the English alphabet, with some modifications to represent sounds for which there is no equivalent English symbol. The letters used are given below.

Symbol	How to make the sound	Word	Meaning
Consonants			

(Note: b, ch, f, g, h, j, k, l, m, n, p, r, s, sh, v, y and z are more or less as in English)

Symbol	How to make the sound	Word	Meaning
t	put the tongue against the teeth	*tiin*	three
d	tongue against teeth	*do*	two
T	turn the tongue back against the roof of the mouth	*beTii*	daughter
D	tongue back against the roof of the mouth	*DaakTar*	doctor
R	tongue back against the roof of the mouth	*laRii*	girl
Kh	like 'ch' in Scottish 'loch'	*buKhaar*	fever
h	as well as representing the consonant 'h' and combining with 'ch' and 'sh' more or less as it does in English (and with '*Kh*' indicated above), 'h' also shows when a sound is 'said with breath'. Compare *beTii* meaning 'daughter', where the '*T*' is not 'breathy' with *Thiik* meaning 'fine' where it is. And compare *chaar* meaning 'four' with *chhai* meaning 'six'.		

Note There are sometimes double consonants in Hindi/Urdu words. For instance, in *bachchaa*, meaning 'child', the '*ch*' is doubled. In *achchhaa* meaning 'good', the '*ch*' is doubled and the second '*ch*' is said with breath as well.

Vowels

aa	a 'long' sound, like the a in English 'father'	*aap*	you
a	'short', like u in English 'up'	*das*	ten
ii	'long', like ee in English 'queen'	*beTii*	daughter
i	'short' like i in English 'ink'	*din*	day
uu	'long' like oo in English 'pool'	*puuraa*	full
u	'short' like u in English 'put'	*guTnaa*	knee
e	represents the sound 'e' as in Hindi/Urdu	*meraa*	my
ai	together represent the sound 'ai' in Hindi/Urdu	*hai*	is
o	represents the sound 'o' as in Hindi/Urdu	*do*	two
au	represent the sound 'au' as in Hindi/Urdu	*aur*	and

Nasality

~	shows where a vowel is pronounced through the nose and mouth together, not just through the mouth	*nahĩĩ*	no

It is worth noting that neither the Hindi nor Urdu scripts use capital letters and similarly the 'English' script used here does not use capitals at the beginning of sentences or for names, except in the English translations.

How to use this course

Read and practise the key expressions at the beginning of each unit. Then read aloud the conversations which you'll also find are recorded on the cassette. (The cassette covers the same language features as this book, but in a slightly different way, so that it can be used independently of the book, while driving a car for instance.) The new language features and any words appearing in the conversations for the first time are explained in the 'Explanations' section. Then listen to the conversations again without the book, and work through the exercises. At the end of the course see how well you have got on by trying the 'Can you get by?' exercises at the end of the book.

12 baaraa

1 Greetings and courtesies

Key expressions

namaste or *namaskar*	Hindu greeting and reply
assalaam alaikum	Muslim greeting
vaalaikum salaam	Reply to Muslim greeting
sat srii akaal	Sikh greeting and reply
Khudaa haafiz	Muslim goodbye
halo/halo jii	Hello
guDbaaii	Goodbye
aapkaa kyaa haal hai?	How are you?
shukriiyaa, mãi Thiik hũu	Thanks, I'm fine

Conversations

(The superior numbers refer to the explanations given below)

1 Helen greets Munir Begum

HELEN   assalaam alaikum.
MUNIR   vaalaikum salaam.[1]

2 Helen greets Amrita Kaur

HELEN   sat srii akaal.
AMRITA   sat srii akaal.[1]

3 Peter greets Raj Sharma

PETER   namaste.
RAJ   namaste.[1]

4 Mohan Singh greets Akbar Ali and asks how he is

MOHAN   halo jii.[2]
AKBAR   halo.
MOHAN   aapkaa kyaa haal hai?[3]
AKBAR   shukriiyaa, mãi Thiik hũu. aur[4] aapkaa kyaa haal hai?
MOHAN   mãi bhii [5] Thiik hũu, shukriiyaa.

5 Naseem has just been introduced to Shameem

NASEEM   assalaam alaikum.
SHAMEEM   vaalaikum salaam.
NASEEM   aap se milkar baRii Khushii huii.[6]
SHAMEEM   aap se milkar bhii bahut Khushii huii.

6 Peter is having a meal at Akbar's house

AKBAR   khaanaa kaisaa lagaa?[7]
PETER   khaanaa bahut achchhaa hai.[7]
AKBAR   shukriiyaa.

7 Peter is leaving Akbar's house

PETER   ijaazat diijiiye.[8]
AKBAR   achchhaa. Khudaa haafiz.
PETER   Khudaa haafiz. phir milẽge.[9]

Explanations

1 Greetings

These vary according to whether the speakers are Muslim, Hindus or Sikhs.

Muslims greet one another with *assalaam alaikum,* literally 'Peace be upon you' and in response say *vaalaikum salaam,* or *vaalaikum assalaam*, 'Peace be upon you too'.

Sikhs say *sat srii akaal,* literally 'Truth is eternal' and the reply is the same.

Hindus say *namaste,* or *namaskar* literally 'Respect to you' and the reply is the same.

If you <u>know</u> the religion of the person you are addressing you can use the appropriate greeting, as Helen did in greeting Munir Begum, a Muslim, and in greeting Amrita Kaur, a Sikh and as Peter did in greeting Raj Sharma, a Hindu. But if you are at all unsure what someone's religion is its best to say *halo,* or *halo jii*, just as Mohan Singh (a Sikh) did in greeting Akbar Ali (a Muslim). This is exactly what Hindu/Urdu speakers do when they don't know someone's religion or if they want to avoid religious connotations. Hindi/Urdu speakers themselves can generally tell whether someone is a Muslim, Hindu or Sikh from their name, because, as you will see in the next unit, Muslim, Hindu and Sikh names are quite distinct. Even so many prefer to just say *halo*.

When English speakers would say 'goodbye', Hindus and Sikhs use the same words used for greeting people, *namaste* and *sat srii akaal*, while Muslims say *Khudaa haafiz*, literally 'God protect'. But, as with the greetings, Hindi/Urdu speakers also use *guDbai* where they wish to avoid religious connotations. Television and radio programmes for south Asian audiences also use *halo* and *guDbai*.

2 *jii*
This is sometimes added to greetings, the words for relatives, and to names to convey respect. For example:

namaste jii
assalaam alaikum bahan jii (*bahan* means 'sister')

3 How are you?
Greetings are nearly always followed by asking how someone is.

aapkaa kyaa haal hai? means literally 'your what condition is?' i.e. 'what is your condition?' The question is often shortened to *kyaa haal hai?* This question is the same whether you are asking a man or a woman. (There is another way of asking, 'How are you?' which you will meet in Unit 5, where you will also meet variations of the 'Thanks, I'm fine' answer.)

The reply *shukriiyaa, māĩ Thiik hūũ* means literally 'thanks, I fine am', i.e. 'thanks, I'm fine'. *shukriiyaa* means 'thank you' or 'thanks'.

People also sometimes reply by simply saying *Thiik hūũ,* meaning 'fine am', i.e, 'I'm fine'. This is a shortened form of *māĩ Thiik hūũ,* the *māĩ* (I) being understood. They also sometimes reply *Thiik hai* meaning 'fine is', i.e. 'It's fine'. This is actually a shortened form of *meraa haal Thiik hai,* which means 'my condition is fine'..Again the *meraa haal* is understood.

4 *aur*
This means 'and'.

5 *bhii*
This means 'also'.

6 *aap se milkar baRii Khushii huii*
This means 'Very pleased to meet you', (literally, 'having-met you, great happiness is'.) You say this on meeting someone. You will also hear *aap se milkar bahut Khushii huii; bahut* means 'very' or 'a lot'.

7 *khaanaa kaisaa lagaa?* ('How was the food?') or
khaanaa bahut achchhaa hai
'The food is very good' (literally, 'food very good is'). You might want to say this about a meal. *achchhaa* here means 'good'. (You will meet it again used in a different way in Unit 4.)

8 *ijaazat diijiiye*
'May I go? (literally 'please give permission'). This is a polite way of saying 'I have to leave now', which you might use after having a meal with Hindi/Urdu speaking friends for example. They may reply, as Akbar does, by saying *achchhaa* meaning 'right!', or perhaps by saying, 'Really, do you have to go?' and try to persuade you to stay a little longer!

9 *phir milēge*
'We'll meet again' i.e. 'See you again'

Exercises

1 Look at the three short conversations. Are the greetings Hindu, Muslim or Sikh?

(a) SPEAKER 1   sat srii akaal.
     SPEAKER 2   sat srii akaal.
(b) SPEAKER 1   namaste.
     SPEAKER 2   namaste.
(c) SPEAKER 1   assalaam alaikum.
     SPEAKER 2   vaalaikum salaam.

2 What would you say if:

(a) You meet a Muslim friend
(b) You meet an Hindi/Urdu speaker but don't know their religion
(c) You meet a Hindu friend
(d) You are introduced to a Sikh colleague.

3 How do you say:

(a) Hello, how are you? (to someone whose religion you don't know)
(b) Thanks, I'm fine

4 Fill in the gaps

(a) RAJ halo aabid, ... kyaa . . . . hai?
     ABID . . . . , mãi, ... huũ.
(b) ABID aur aapkaa, ... hai?
     RAJ   . . . Thiik . . . , shukriiyaa.

5 Complete the speech bubbles:

(a)

(b)

20 biis

2 Names

Key expressions

meraa naam Sue hai	My name is Sue
aapkaa naam kyaa hai?	What is your name?
meraa puuraa naam	
nasiim begum hai	My full name is Naseem Begum
aapkaa puuraa naam kyaa hai?	What is your full name?
aapkaa puuraa naam . . . . . hai?	Is your full name . . . . ?
jii hãã	Yes
jii nahĩĩ	No
jii hãã, meraa puuraa naam . . . hai.	Yes, my full name is . . . .

Conversations

1 Sue and Raj introduce themselves

SUE   halo! meraa naam Sue hai.[1]
RAJ   halo! meraa naam raaj hai.[1]

2 Abid meets Sue and Raj

ABID   halo! meraa naam aabid hai. aapkaa naam kyaa hai?
SUE   meraa naam Sue hai.
ABID   aur aapkaa naam kyaa hai?[2]
RAJ   meraa naam raaj hai.

Abid finds out Raj's and Sue's full names

ABID   meraa puuraa naam aabid alii Khaan hai.
raaj, aapkaa puuraa naam kyaa hai?

RAJ   meraa puuraa naam raaj sharmaa hai.

ABID   aur Sue, aapkaa puuraa naam kyaa hai?

SUE   meraa puuraa naam Sue Hardy hai.

4 Helen checks Naseem's name

HELEN   meraa naam Helen hai. aapkaa naam nasiim hai?[3]

NASEEM   jii hãã [4], meraa naam nasiim hai.

HELEN   aur aapkaa puuraa naam nasiim begum [5] 'hai?

NASEEM   jii hãã, meraa puuraa naam nasiim begum hai.

5 Anna, a dentist's receptionist, finds out which Mr Singh she's talking to

ANNA   halo, aapkaa naam singh [6] hai?

MR SINGH   jii hãã.

ANNA   aapkaa puuraa naam armindar singh hai?

MR SINGH   jii nahĩĩ [4], meraa puuraa naam ranjiit singh hai.

Explanations

1 My name

e.g. *meraa naam Anna hai*
    meraa naam Peter hai
literally 'my name . . . is'.

2 What is your name?

The question is the same whether you are asking a
man or a woman: *aapkaa naam kyaa hai?*, literally,
'Your name what is?'.

3 Asking questions

There are two main ways to ask a question:
(a) you simply use a rising tone in your voice.

aapkaa naam paramjiit hai	Your name is Paramjeet
aapkaa naam paramjiit hai?	Is your name Paramjeet?
aapkaa puuraa naam raaj sharmaa hai?	Is your full name Raj Sharma?

(b) sometimes Hindi/Urdu speakers add the word
kyaa? (what?) before a sentence:

kyaa, aapkaa naam paramjiit hai?
kyaa, aapkaa puuraa naam raaj sharmaa hai?

4 Yes and no: *jii hāā* and *jii nahīī*

The ¯ over the top indicates that the *hāā* in *jii hāā*
and the *nahīī* in *jii nahīī* are pronounced not just
through the mouth but through the mouth and
nose together – the sound is nasalised. You'll
meet other nasalised sounds too, as the sign ¯ will
show.

5 *begum*

This is a female title used by Muslim women which follows the first name. It means something like 'lady' or 'Mrs' and should not really be used as a surname although this often happens when names are written down, for example, in medical records. See 'What's in a name' below.

6 *singh*

This is a religious title used by Sikh men following their first name. It indicates that the man is a Sikh. *singh* is actually a Punjabi word meaning 'lion'. It is not traditionally a surname but it is sometimes used as one in Britain. See 'What's in a name' below.

Exercises

1 Answer these questions:
(a) aapkaa naam kyaa hai?
(b) aapka puuraa naam kyaa hai?

2 Ask:
(a) What is your name?
(b) What is your full name?
(c) Is your name Aziz?

3 Fill in the gaps:
(a) RAJ   halo, ... naam . . . . hai?
    ABID   . . . . aabid . . .
(b) SUE   aapkaa . . . . parviin . . . ?
    PARVEEN . . . . . . , meraa naam parviin hai.

4 What is the Hindi/Urdu for the following:
(a) What is your name?
(b) My name is Helen.
(c) Is your full name Helen Allen?
(d) Yes, my full name is Helen Allen.
(e) No, my name is not Rajeev, my name is Raj.

What's in a name

Hindu, Muslim and Sikh names are different from each other as well as from English names. For example, first names may not tell you whether the person is a man or a woman. It's generally a good idea to ask for someone's <u>full</u> name before writing their name for example, in medical records or class registers.

Muslim names

Muslim families don't have a tradition of surnames and family members may have different names, though in Britain some families have begun using a shared surname.

● <u>A man's name</u> usually has two or three parts. If the first name is a religious name, such as Mohammad (*muhammad*) or Allah (*allaah*), it is usually used together with the second name, e.g. Mohammad Safdar (*muhammad safdar*), Allah Bakhsh (*allah baKhsh*); most Muslims find it offensive to use the religious name alone.

● <u>Muslim women</u> usually have two names, a personal name and a second name. This second name is either a female title or a second personal name and the two names are often used together, e.g. Fatima Jan (*faatimaa jaan*), Naseem Akhtar (*nasiim aKhtar*). If the second name is a female title then you'll see Bibi (*biibii*), Khatoon (*Khaatuun*), Bi (*bii*) and Begum (*begum*) used.

● <u>Some women in Britain</u> are now using their husband's last name as a shared family name, e.g. Amina (*amiinaa*) Begum married to Muhammad Aslam becomes Amina Begum Aslam (*amiinaa begum aslaam*) in British records. In formal situations Muslims may say 'Sahib' (*saahib*) to a man, or 'Sahiba' (*saahibaa*), to a woman, after the personal name, e.g. Akbar Sahib (*akbar saahib*), Nafisa Sahiba (*nafiisaa saahibaa*).

Hindu names

Hindus usually have one or more personal names and a family name, e.g. Raj Kumar Sharma (*raaj kumaar sharmaa*), for a man; Usha Devi Sharma (*ushaa devii sharmaa*) for a woman. In a formal situation, Hindus may say Shri to a man <u>before</u>, or Sahib <u>after</u> the second or the full name e.g. Sunil Chand would be spoken to as Shri Chand or Chand Sahib. To be polite to a married woman, Hindus say Shrimati before her first or her full name, e.g. Shrimati Nirmala Devi (*shriimatii nirmalaa devii*).

Sikh names

Sikh names have three parts, a personal name, a religious name and a family name. Traditionally Sikhs don't use the family name, but in Britain some are now using it as a surname. The middle name is the religious name, showing that the person is a Sikh. Women use 'Kaur' (meaning 'princess') and men use 'Singh'. Sometimes, these religious names are used as a surname.

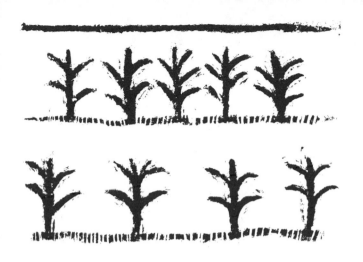

3 Family

Key expressions

aap shaadii-shudaa hãi?	Are you married
aapke bachche hãi?	Do you have children?
kitne?	How many?
meraa ek beTaa hai	I have one son
mere do beTe hãi	I have two sons
merii ek beTii hai	I have one daughter
merii do beTiiyãã hãi	I have two daughters
aapke kitne beTe hãi?	How many sons do you have?
aapkii kitnii beTiiyãã hãi?	How many daughters do you have?

Conversations

1 Mary, an English teacher, meets Nisha and asks if she is married and has children

MARY   nishaa, aap shaadii-shudaa [1] hãi?[2]

NISHA   jii hãã, mãi shaadii-shudaa hũũ. [1]

MARY   aapke bachche hãi?[3]

NISHA   jii hãã, mere bachche hãi.

MARY   kitne?

NISHA   mere tiin [4] bachche hãi.
meraa ek beTaa hai aur merii do beTiyãã hãi. [5]

2 Shameem asks Mary if she is married and has children

SHAMEEM   Mary, aap shaadii-shudaa hãi?

MARY   jii hãã, mãi shaadii-shudaa hũũ.

SHAMEEM   aur aapke bachche hãi?

MARY   jii hãã, mere tiin bachche hãi.
merii ek beTii hai aur do beTe hãi.[5]

3 Kaniz asks Helen how many children she has

KANIZ   Helen, aapke kitne bachche hãi?
HELEN   mere chaar bachche hãi.
KANIZ   aapkii beTiiyãā kitnii hãi?[6]
HELEN   merii do beTiiyãā hãi.
KANIZ   aur aapke do beTe hãi?
HELEN   jii hãā, mere do beTe hãi.

4 Anna visits Kirpal's family and meets his wife and children

KIRPAL   ye [7] merii patnii hãi.
ANNA   halo, aap se milkar baRii Khushii huii.
KIRPAL   ye merii chhoTii [8] beTii harpaal hai.
   ye meraa baRaa [9] beTaa balbiir hai.
   aur ye mera choTaa beTaa avtaar hai.

5 Helen meets Akbar's wife and daughters

AKBAR   ye merii bivii hãi.
HELEN   halo. aap se milkar baRii Khushii huii.
AKBAR   aur ye merii beTiiyãā hãi.
   ye merii choTii beTii parviin hai.
   aur ye merii baRii beTii nasiim hai.

Explanations

1 *shaadii-shudaa*

This means 'married'. The question *aap shaadii-shudaa hãi?* in effect implies 'are you married yet?'; the assumption is that under normal circumstances marriage happens inevitably to everyone, and it is generally assumed that children will follow as quickly as possible. It is very unusual in south Asian society for someone unmarried to have children. The reply *mãi shaadii-shudaa hũū* means literally, 'I married am' i.e. 'I am married'. Note the pronunciation of *mãi* meaning 'I' and of *hũū* meaning 'am' – both words are nasalised.

2 hai and hāi

So far you have met *hai*, not *hāi*, e.g.

aapkaa kyaa haal hai?   Your what state is? i.e.
                              How are you?

aapkaa naam kyaa hai? Your name what is? i.e.
                              What is your name?

hai means 'is' and *hāi* means 'are'

But *hāi* is also used courteously about one person, someone of equal or senior status, to show respect. You say *hāi* with *aap* ('you') because *aap* is the formal 'you'. The difference in sound between *hai* and *hāi* is that *hāi* is nasalised.

3 aapke bachche hāi?

Literally 'Your children are?' i.e. 'Do you have children?'

bachche meaning 'children' is the plural of *bachchaa*, 'child'. Note the *hāi*, meaning 'are'. You use *hāi* when you talk about more than one child and *hai* when talking about one child. Here are some examples:

meraa ek bachchaa hai	My one child is i.e. I have one child (a boy)
merii ek bachchii hai	My one child is i.e. I have one child (a girl)
mere do bachche hāi	My two children are i.e. I have two children

4 tiin

This means 'three'. You will find all the numbers from 0 to a million in the appendix. But here are the numbers from 1 – 10:

1	*ek*	6	*chhai*
2	*do*	7	*saat*
3	*tiin*	8	*aaTh*
4	*chaar*	9	*nau*
5	*pāach*	10	*das*

5 Nouns and their plurals

Hindi/Urdu words for people or things (nouns) are either masculine or feminine. As in English, the endings of nouns usually change according to their number e.g. one child (singular), two children (plural). Unlike English, the endings also vary for masculine and feminine nouns, e.g.:

	Singular	Plural
beTaa	*ek beTaa*	*do beTe*
	one son	two sons
beTii	*ek beTii*	*do beTiiyā̃*
	one daughter	two daughters

In Hindi/Urdu, many masculine nouns end in *-aa* when singular and in *-e* when plural, and many feminine nouns end in *-ii* when singular and in *-iiyā̃* when plural.

The endings of the adjectives *meraa* (my), and *aapkaa* (your) also change. With masculine singular nouns they end in *-aa*, with masculine plural nouns they end in *-e*, and they end in *-ii* with all feminine nouns. For example:

Singular	Plural
meraa beTaa	*mere beTe*
merii beTii	*merii beTiiyā̃*

Other adjectives (describing words like 'big' and 'little' etc.) change in this way too.

6 *kitne?* how many

This is also an adjective and so it changes too. In asking how many sons or daughters someone has you'd say:

aapke kitne beTe hā̃?	How many sons do you have? (literally 'Your how many sons are?')
aapkii kitnii beTiiyā̃ hā̃?	How many daughters do you have? (literally 'Your how many daughters are?')

Hindi/Urdu speakers sometimes change the order of words: *aapkii beTiiyãã kitnii hãĩ?*

7 *ye*
This means 'he', 'she', 'they' 'this' or 'these'. For example:

ye meraa beTaa hai	This is my son
ye merii beTii hai	This is my daughter
ye mere bachche hãĩ	These are my children
ye meraa naam hai	This is my name

8 *chhoTaa*
This means 'small', 'little' or 'younger'.

9 *baRaa*
This means 'big', or 'elder'.

mãi shaadii-shudaa nahĩĩ hũũ	I am not married
ye kaun hai?	Who is this/he/she? (about someone junior)
ye kaun hãĩ?	Who is he/she? (about someone of equal or senior status, to whom you are showing respect: note the courteous *'hãĩ'*) or Who are these?
ek laRkii	one girl
ek laRkaa	one boy
do laRkiiyãã	two girls
do laRke	two boys
patnii	wife (Hindi only)
patii	husband (Hindi only)
biivii	wife (Urdu only)
shauhar	husband (Urdu only)
baap	father
mãã	mother
daadaa	grandfather (paternal)
daadii	grandmother (paternal)
naanaa	grandfather (maternal)
naanii	grandmother (maternal)
susar	father-in-law
saas	mother-in-law
bhaaii	brother
bahan	sister

Exercises

1 Ask:
(a) Are you married?
(b) Do you have children?
(c) How many children do you have?
(d) How many daughters do you have?
(e) How many sons do you have?

2 You are Amrita Kaur, married with four children, two sons and two daughters. Now answer the questions given in 1 above.

3 You are Akbar Ahmed, married with six children, five sons and one daughter. Answer the questions given in 1 above.

4 You are Rashmi Shankar, married with three daughters and one son. Answer the questions given in 1 above.

5 Write the questions to which the following are answers:
(a) jii hāā, mãĩ shaadii-shudaa hũu.
(b) jii hāā, mere chaar bachche hãĩ.
(c) ye merii choTii beTii hai.
(d) mere chaar bachche hãĩ.
(e) jii hāā, meraa ek beTaa hai.
(f) jii nahĩĩ, merii do beTiiyãā hãĩ.

Worth knowing

The extended family is very important in south Asian society and in Britain it is still quite common for a married son to live with his wife and children in his parents' house, or for two brothers and their wives and children to share one house. Cousins often refer to and address each other as *bhaaii* (brother) or *bahan* (sister), rather than by the Hindi/Urdu words which specify exactly which kind of cousin they are. This can often be confusing to health visitors and teachers! A close friend who is not a relative may also be addressed as *bhaaii* or *bahan*, or *Khaalaa* (mother's sister) or *chachaa* (father's brother), depending on their age and status. It is important to show respect to those who are older and senior, not just within the family, as the language in this unit has shown, but outside it too.

Many westerners are interested in the question of caste in Hindu society. There are thousands of castes in India which traditionally fall into four main groups: Brahmins (priests), Kshatriyas (warriors and aristocrats), Vaishyas (farmers and tradesmen) and Shudras (labourers), with the untouchables, now called Harijans, falling outside this grouping. A person's family name may indicate their caste background. But today caste is not always linked to occupation, and it is virtually impossible to say anything definite about it, as attitudes towards caste differ so much from one community to another. The feelings associated with caste in Hindu society are very like those associated with social class in the West; it's really a question of social status. For instance, parents prefer children to marry within the caste, and feel a loss of status if a daughter marries someone of lower caste.

Unlike Hinduism, Islam believes in the equality of all and that differences of status don't have any religious significance. Many Muslims in India and Pakistan are descendants of Hindus who converted to Islam to escape the caste system. But the significance of caste among Muslims in India and Pakistan is still much debated. Family names often indicate caste background, and there is a status hierarchy of Muslim families. Originally this was linked to traditional occupations, with descendants of the Prophet and his family, and also of Muslim invaders and rulers, all having high status. The Muslims' concern that marriage takes place within the extended family, and their preference for cousin marriage, tends to maintain the exclusivity of particular families.

The Sikhs, whose religion stemmed from an attempt by Guru Nanak in the 16th century to bridge Hinduism and Islam, are, like the Muslims, theoretically opposed to giving caste any religious significance, and the religion originally attracted many converts from Hinduism. But, as with the Muslims, differences within the Sikh population often reflect caste, as well as class, distinctions, and caste is still crucial in marriage arrangements.

4 Where you work and live

Key expressions

maĩ soshal varkar huũ	I am (a) social worker
aap kyaa kaam kartii haĩ?	What work do you do? (fem.)
aap kyaa kaam karte haĩ?	What work do you do? (masc.)
maĩ Tiichar nahĩĩ huũ	I am not (a) teacher
maĩ . . . mẽ kaam kartii huũ	I work in . . . (fem.)
aap kahãã kaam kartii haĩ?	Where do you work? (fem.)
aap kahãã kaam karte haĩ?	Where do you work? (masc.)
maĩ . . . mẽ kaam kartaa huũ	I work in . . . (masc.)
maĩ . . . mẽ rahtii huũ	I live in . . . (fem.)
aap kahãã rahtii haĩ?	Where do you live? (fem.)
aap kahãã rahte haĩ?	Where do you live? (masc.)
maĩ . . . mẽ rahtaa huũ	I live in . . . (masc.)
aapkaa pataa kyaa hai?	What is your address?
meraa pataa . . . . . . roD hai	My address is . . . . . . road.
aapkaa Teliifon nambar kyaa hai?	What is your telephone number?
meraa Teliffon nambar . . . . . . hai	My telephone number is . . . . . .

Conversations

1 Helen and Rashmi introduce themselves

HELEN   halo, meraa naam Helen hai.
aur mãi ek soshal varkar hũu.[1]

RASHMI   halo, meraa naam rashmii hai.
mãi Tiichar hũu. [1]

2 Shamim finds out what work Helen and Tariq do

SHAMIM   Helen, aap kyaa kaam kartii hãi?[2]

HELEN   mãi soshal varkar hũu.

SHAMIM   aur taariq, aap kyaa kaam karte hãi?[2]

TARIQ   mãi Tiichar hũu.

3 Peter asks what Radha does

PETER   raadhaa, app Tiichar hãi?

RADHA   jii nahĩĩ, mãi Tiichar nahĩĩ hũu[3],
akaunTanT hũu.

4 Shamim tells Helen and Tariq about her job and asks them about theirs

SHAMIM   mãi nars hũu.
aur janral haspiTaal mẽ kaam kartii hũu.[4]
taariq, aap kahãã[5] kaam karte hãi?

TARIQ   mãi haaii skuul mẽ kaam kartaa hũu.[4]

SHAMIM   aur Helen? aap kahãã kaam kartii hãi?

HELEN   mãi sytii santar mẽ kaam kartii hũu

5 Raj asks Naseem where she lives

RAJ   nasiim, aap kahãã rahtii hãi?[6]

NASEEM   mãi Manchester mẽ rahtii hũu.

6 Naseem asks Raj where he lives

NASEEM   raaj, aap kahãã rahte hãi?[6]

RAJ   mãi bhii [7] Manchester mẽ rahtãã hũu.

NASEEM   achchhaa! [8] Manchester mẽ kahãã . . . ?

RAJ   mãi Salford mẽ rahtaa hũu.

7 Helen asks Tariq for his address

HELEN   aapkaa pataa kyaa hai?[9]
TARIQ   meraa pataa solaa griin roD hai.
HELEN   achchhaa. shukriiyaa.

8 Naseem and Raj exchange phone numbers

NASEEM   aapkaa Teliifon nambar kyaa hai?[10]
RAJ   meraa Teliifon nambar 246930 hai.
    aur aapkaa Teliifon nambar kyaa hai?
NASEEM   meraa? meraa Teliifon nambar 614500
    hai.
RAJ   614500 hai?
NASEEM   jii hãã.
RAJ   achchhaa. shukriiyaa.

Explanations

1 *mãi . . . . hũũ*

Literally means 'I . . . . am', and is the same for a
male or a female speaker. For describing
occupations, Hindi/Urdu speakers in Britain often
use English words adapted to Hindi/Urdu
pronunciation, for example, *mãi Tiichar hũũ* 'I am
a teacher'.

2 What work do you do?

karnaa is the verb 'to do' and *kaam* means 'work',
so *kaam karnaa* is 'to do work'.

If you are asking a woman you say, *aap kyaa kaam
kartii hãi?* (literally 'you what work do?'). If you're
asking a man, it's *aap kyaa kaam karte hãi?*

As you can see, *kartii* has *-ii* on the end when
you're talking to a woman. *karte* has *-e* on the end
when you're talking to a man. In both cases the
hãi is nasalised; this shows respect. Look at the
order of words too: the verb comes at the end of
the sentence, which is typical of Hindi/Urdu.

3 How to say 'no'

To make a sentence negative, put *nahĩĩ* in front of the verb, e.g.

meraa naam Mick nahĩĩ hai	My name is not Mick
mãĩ shaadii-shudaa nahĩĩ hũũ	I am not married
mãĩ Tiichar nahĩĩ hũũ	I am not a teacher

To say 'no' to a question you can either just say *jii nahĩĩ*, or start your answer with *jii nahĩĩ* and then put *nahĩĩ* in front of the verb.

4 I work in . . .

A woman says:	*mãĩ . . . mẽ kaam kartii hũũ*
A man says:	*mãĩ . . . mẽ kaam kartaa hũũ*

When a man is speaking about himself, he uses the masculine singular *-aa* ending of *kartaa*; you don't use the respectful plural *-e* ending if you're talking about yourself!

mẽ means 'in', and always comes after what it refers to, e.g.

janral haspiTaal mẽ	in the general hospital
haaii skuul mẽ	in the high school

For places too Hindi/Urdu speakers in Britain often use English words adapted to Hindi/Urdu pronunciation.

5 Where do you work?

kahãã means 'where?'

If you're asking a woman, you say: *aap kahãã kaam kartii hãĩ?* literally 'you (fem.) where work do?'. If you're asking a man, you say: *aap kahãã kaam karte hãĩ?*

Here again, notice the *-ii* ending for a woman and the *-e* ending for a man.

6 Where do you live?

rahnaa is the verb 'to live'

You ask a woman *aap kahãã rahtii hãĩ?*, literally 'you where live?' and a man *aap kahãã rahte hãĩ?*

The reply, for a woman, is: *mãĩ . . . mẽ rahtii hũũ*, literally 'I . . . in live', and for a man: *mãĩ . . . mẽ rahtaa hũũ*

Note the -*aa* ending for a man.

7 bhii

You have already met *bhii* in Unit 1, meaning 'also', so *mãĩ bhii Manchester mẽ rahtaa hũũ* means literally 'I also Manchester in live', i.e. I also live in Manchester. In English it doesn't matter whether you say 'I live in Manchester too', or 'I also live in Manchester' but in Hindi/Urdu *bhii* must come directly after who or what it refers to or the meaning changes. For instance, *mãĩ Manchester mẽ bhii rahtaa hũũ* means 'I live in Manchester as well as somewhere else' i.e. I have two homes.

8 achchhaa

This again you met in Unit 1, where it meant good. Here it means something like 'I see', or 'right'. It shows that the speaker has registered what she was told. With a question intonation *achchhaa?* means 'really?', and with an exclamation it can indicate surprise: *achchhaa!*

9 pataa

This literally means 'clue' or 'trace'. Hindi/Urdu speakers in Britain also use the English word 'address'.

10 Telephone numbers.

You will find all the numbers from 0 to 1 million in the appendix. You'll be relieved to know that Hindi/Urdu speakers in Britain often give telephone and house numbers in English.

Word list

berozgaar	unemployed
dukaan mē	in (a) shop
DaakTar	doctor
ghar mē	in/at home
helth vizitar	health visitor
kaar varkar	car worker
midvaaif	midwife
puliismain	policeman

Exercises

1 You are Kamaljiit Kaur, a social worker. How would you answer these questions?
(a) aapkaa naam kyaa hai?
(b) aap kyaa kaam kartii hāı?

2 You are Peter Harris, an accountant. How would you answer these questions?
(a) aapkaa naam kyaa hai?
(b) aap kyaa kaam karte hāı?

3 You are meeting Parveen for the first time. Ask her name and what she does.

4 You are meeting Ravi for the first time. Ask his name and what he does.

5 Fill in the gaps:
JUNE Ann, aap DaakTar . . . ?
ANN   jii nahīı, māı . . . . hūu. māı
      akaunTanT . . .

6 Ask each person where they live, and then give their reply.
Example:
Shamim Begum, London
Shamim, aap kahā̃ rahtii hāı?
māı London mē rahtii hūu.

(a) Naseem Sahib, Coventry
(b) Usha Devi, Birmingham
(c) Amina Begum, Glasgow
(d) Amrita Kaur, London
(e) Raj Kumar, Delhi
(f) Jenny, Manchester
(g) Amrit Singh, Walsall
(h) Bob, Derby

7 You are a doctor's receptionist. Amina Begum wants to register with the doctor. Ask her:
(a) her full name
(b) where she lives
(c) her telephone number
(d) her occupation

Worth knowing

The places in Britain where Hindi/Urdu speakers
live and work reflect to a large extent where they
lived before leaving for Britain and their reasons
for leaving. Most of the Pakistani Muslims, for
instance, who are from rural Punjab and Mirpur in
Azad Kashmir, came to Britain to look for work in
the late 1950s and early 1960s. They settled in the
West Midlands, West Yorkshire, Lancashire,
Staffordshire and Scotland, where there were
labour shortages, mainly in the manufacturing
industries, steelworks and textile mills. Some of
them moved to the south-east later. Once a man
had found work, he tended to be joined by
relatives and friends from the same part of
Pakistan. Today, Bradford, Birmingham and
Glasgow for instance have significant Pakistani
populations.

Britain's Indian population is on the whole
scattered more evenly throughout Britain than the
Pakistani population. The Indian Punjabis have
settled mostly in London, Middlesex (notably
Southall), Surrey and the Midlands. They are
predominantly Jat Sikhs from rural Punjab who
came to Britain at roughly the same time as the
majority of Pakistani Muslims and for much the
same reasons. The Indian Hindu population has
settled throughout the south-east and the
Midlands. The East African Sikhs, Gujaratis and
Hindus came to Britain in the late 1970s and early
1980s for very different reasons. Technically
skilled, more middle class and relatively
prosperous, they have settled in most of Britain's
large cities, rather than concentrated in inner city
areas, and tend to work in middle-level
administration, businesses or the professions.

5 Health

Key expressions

aap kaisii hãĩ?	How are you (fem.)?
aap kaise hãĩ?	How are you (masc.)?
mãĩ Thiik nahĩĩ hũũ	I am not OK
mãĩ biimaar hũũ	I am ill
kyaa baat hai?	What's the matter?
mujhe (bahut) dard hai	I have (a lot of) pain
mujhe buKhaar hai	I have a fever/ temperature
mujhe zukaam hai	I have a cold
mujhe khaansii hai	I have a cough
aapko dard hai?	Do you have pain?
dard kahãã hai?	Where is the pain?
dard yahãã hai	The pain is here
dard sar mẽ hai	The pain is in (the) head.
mere peT mẽ dard hai	(There) is pain in my stomach
mujhe . . . . dikhaaiiye	Please show me . . . .

Conversations

1 Ahmed meets his friend Raj

AHMED   raaj, aap kaise hãĩ?[1]
RAJ   mãĩ Thiik nahii hũũ, bhaaii.
AHMED   kyaa baat hai?
RAJ   mujhe zukaam hai.[2]
AHMED   aur buKhaar bhii hai?
RAJ   jii hãã, buKhaar bhii hai, aur khaansii bhii hai.
AHMED   achchhaa! aapkaa DaakTar kaun hai?
RAJ   DaakTar jons hai.
AHMED   aap DaakTar ke paas[3] jaaiiye![4]

2 Sita is at the doctor's surgery

DOCTOR	aaiiyee[4] baiThiiye.[4]
	kyaa baat hai?
SITA	mere kaan mẽ bahut dard hai[5], DaakTar saahibaa.
DOCTOR	achchhaa. mujhe kaan dikhaaiiye to.[4]
	(looks at her ear)
	gale mẽ bhii dard hai, kyaa?
SITA	jii hãã.
DOCTOR	achchhaa! hãã! (feeling her throat) gale mẽ sojan lagtii hai.[6]

3 The doctor tells Sita not to worry

DOCTOR	aap fikr naa kiijiiye. aapkaa kaan ek do din mẽ Thiik hojaaegaa.[7]
	dard ke liiye[8] ek do asprin khaaliijiiye.[4]

4 Amrita goes to the doctor

DOCTOR	aaiiye! baiThiiye! aap kaisii hãĩ?
AMRITA	mãĩ Thiik nahĩĩ hũũ.
	mere peT mẽ bahut dard hai.
DOCTOR	achchhaa. leT jaaiiye!
	dard yahãã hai? (feeling her stomach)
AMRITA	jii hãã.
DOCTOR	rozaanaa[9] khaane ke baad[10] ek golii khaaiiye.
	aapkaa peT do tiin din mẽ Thiik hojaaegaa.

Explanations

1 *aap kaisii/kaise hãi*

This is another way of asking 'How are you?' which means literally 'you how are?' You say *aap kaisii hãi?* to a woman, *aap kaise hãi?* to a man.

2 *mujhe zukaam hai*

Literally, ' to me (a) cold is' i.e. I have a cold. You can use this to describe how you are feeling. Here are some other examples:

mujhe buKhaar hai	'To-me (a) temperature/fever is' i.e. I have a temperature/fever.
mujhe khaansii hai	'To-me a cough is' i.e. I have a cough
mujhe dard hai	'To-me pain is' i.e. I have a pain

To turn this into a question you would say:

aapko dard hai?	'to-you pain is?' i.e. do you have pain?

3 *ke paas*

Here, this means 'to': 'please go to the doctor!'

4 *jaaiiye*

This is the polite form of the command from the verb *jaanaa*, 'to go'. Similarly, *aaiiye* and *baiThiiye* are polite forms of the verbs *aannaa*, 'to come' and *baiThnaa*, 'to sit down'. The phrase *aaiiye, baiThiiye* is the polite way of saying, 'Come in and sit down'. *dikhaaiiye* and *khaaiiye* are polite forms of the command from the verbs *dikhaanaa*, 'to show', and *khaanaa*, 'to eat'. These polite forms go with *aap* (the courteous 'you'), and the politeness is built in, making words such as 'please' unnecessary. (There is a word for please, *mihrbaanii karke*, which literally means 'doing kindness'. But Hindi/Urdu speakers tend to use this word only when they really do feel that they are asking you a real favour, rather than say it

frequently out of convention as happens with
'please' in English.) These polite commands are
formed by adding -iiye to the root of a verb, e.g.

verb	root	polite command
jaanaa (to go)	jaa	jaaiiye
aanaa (to come)	aa	aaiiye
baiThnaa (to sit down)	baiTh	baiThiiye
dikhaanaa (to show)	dikhaa	dikhaaiiye
khaanaa (to eat)	khaa	khaaiiye

In *dikhaaiije to,* the *to* just means something like
'so', or 'then'. *khaaliijiiye* means the same as
khaaiiye – 'please eat!'.

5 *mere kaan mẽ dard hai*

This means literally 'my ear in pain is' i.e. 'there is
pain in my ear' Similarly, *mere haath mẽ dard hai*
means 'there is pain in my hand' etc. You'll find a
list of parts of the body given in the 'Word list' on
p. 55.

Note that *kaan* is masculine: *meraa kaan*, but
here, because it is followed by the word *mẽ* ('in') it
becomes *mere kaan mẽ*. This is because *mẽ* is a
postposition. (In English we have prepositions,
words such as 'in', 'on', 'from', etc.; in Hindi/Urdu
words like *se* ('from'), *mẽ* ('in') and *ka, ki, ke* ('of')
come after what they refer to.) In Hindi/Urdu
nouns and the adjectives agreeing with them take
special endings when followed by a postposition,
as follows:

Nouns followed by postpositions

Singular	Plural
masc. nouns ending in -aa	
meraa guTnaa (my knee)	mere guTne (my knees)
mere guTne mẽ (in my knee)	mere guTnõ mẽ (in my knees)

masc. nouns not ending in -aa

meraa kaan	*mere kaan*
(my ear)	(my ears)
mere kaan mē	*mere kaanō mē*
(in my ear)	(in my ears)

fem. nouns ending in -ii

merii ūglii	*merii ūgliiyāā*
(my finger)	(my fingers)
merii ūglii mē	*merii ūgliiyō mē*
(in my finger)	(in my fingers)

fem. nouns not ending in -ii

merii Tāāg	*meri Tāāgē**
(my leg)	(my legs)
merii Tāāg mē	*meri Tāāgō me*
(in my leg)	(in my legs)

(*feminine nouns not ending in -ii add *ē* for the plural.)

When followed by postpositions only masculine singular nouns ending in -aa actually change to -e, but adjectives with masculine singular nouns all change -aa to -e, while feminine singular nouns don't change. All plural nouns take the ending -ō when followed by postpositions.

6 *gale mē sojan lagtii hai*

This means 'it seems there's swelling in (your) throat'. 'There *is* swelling in (your) throat' would be *gale mē sojan hai*.

7 *aapkaa kaan ek do din mē Thiik hojaaegaa*

Literally, 'your ear one-two days in fine will be' i.e. 'Your ear will be fine in one or two days.' *hojaaegaa* ends in -aa because it agrees with *kaan*, which is masuculine singular. See how you would use it for other things:

aapkii Tāāg ek do din mē Thiik hojaaegii
aapke (donō) haath ek do din mē Thiik hojaaēge (*donō* means 'both')*aapkii Tāāgē ek do din mē Thiik hojaaēgii*

If you want to say 'You will be fine in one or two days' you say:

aap ek do din mẽ Thiik hojaaẽgii (to a woman)
aap ek do din mẽ Thiik hojaaẽge (to a man)
meaning 'You will be fine in one or two days'.

8 *dard ke liiye*
ke liiye means 'for', and comes after what it refers to, e.g.

dard ke liiye asprin khaaiiye	Eat (i.e. take) asprin for the pain
ye goliiyãã aap ke liiye hãi	These tablets are for you

9 *rozaanaa*
This means 'everyday'.

10 *khaane ke baad*
This means 'after food'.

Word list

khaRe hojaaiiye	Please stand up
leTiiye/leT jaaiiye	Please lie down
fikr naa kiijiiye	Please don't worry
liijiiye	Please take
piijiiye	Please drink
khaaiiye	Please eat
golii (f.)	tablet
davaaii (f.)	medicine
ye davaaii piijiiye	Please drink (i.e. take) this medicine
(ek, do . . .) goliiyãã khaaiiye	Please eat (i.e. take) (one, two,. . .) tablets
paanii piijiiye	Please drink (some) water
mujhe DaakTar chaahiiye	I need a doctor
kyaa ye paanii piine kaa hai?	Is this water drinkable?

Vocabulary for parts of the body

the adjective 'my' is given, to show the gender of the words.

meraa sar	my head
merii ããkh (plural ããkhē)	my eye
merii naak	my nose
meraa kaan	my ear
meraa galaa	my throat
meraa siinaa	my chest
merii baah (plural baahē)	my arm
meraa peT	my stomach
meraa haath	my hand
mere haath kii ūglii	my finger
merii Tããg	my leg
meraa guTnaa	my knee
meraa paaõ	my foot

Exercises

1 You are a doctor. Ask:
(a) a woman how she is
(b) a man how he is
(c) 'What is the matter?'
(d) 'Where is the pain?'

2 You are the patient. The doctor asks: *kyaa baat hai?* Say you have:
(a) a fever
(b) a cough
(c) a cold
(d) pain

3 You have gone to see the doctor. Tell her where the pain is.
Example: Q: *dard kahãã hai?*
       A: (ear)
         dard kaan mẽ hai.
(a) stomach
(b) head
(c) fingers
(d) leg
(e) hand
(f) chest
(g) foot
(h) eyes

4 Fill in the gaps:
HEALTH VISITOR   aap . . . . . . hãi?
SHAMIM BEGUM   mai . . . . . nahĩ . . .
HEALTH VISITOR   kyaa . . . . . hai?
SHAMIM BEGUM   . . . . peT . . dard . . .

5 You are a doctor and need to examine a Hindi/Urdu speaking patient. Ask the patient to show you the following:

Example: Please show me (your) <u>eye</u>
   mujhe āakh dikhaaiiye
- (a) (your) hand
- (b) nose
- (c) throat
- (d) fingers
- (e) leg
- (f) arm
- (g) both arms
- (h) foot

Worth knowing

For Hindi/Urdu speakers in Britain, western medicine and the National Health Service is not the only system of health care they may use. Both in Britain and in India and Pakistan, western medicine is complemented by traditional systems; Unani (Greek) medicine, which is used throughout the Islamic world, and Ayuredic medicine, a traditional medicine of India derived from Indian beliefs. Unani and Ayurvedic medicine is practised widely throughout India and Pakistan. Unani practioners are called hakims, and Ayurvedic practitioners are known as vaids. Some hakims live in Britain, while others visit from India and Pakistan. They advertise their services in the south Asian press, and south Asians often go to see hakims in India or Pakistan during return visits there. They may well go to a hakim as well as to a western doctor, or if they are dissatisfied with or still uncured by western medicine.

Muslims may also consult their imam or priest in such circumstances, and may go to a pir (*piir*). This is a person who is considered to have power to intercede with Allah on someone else's behalf. They may be asked for special prayers or for a tavis (*taaviis*). A tavis is an amulet, worn round the neck, which contains a folded piece of paper on which a pir has written words of the Koran. In cases of extreme and serious illness, people may make return visits to Pakistan or India and visit a pir there or make a pilgramage to the tombs of a deceased pir.

Language and cultural differences can cause problems with making an appropriate diagnosis. There are also cultural differences in the way illness is expressed. For instance western doctors have noticed that south Asian patients tend to express emotional distress by speaking of physical symptoms, like pains in the chest or heart. Saying you have a pain in your heart is one way of saying you are unhappy. Interpreters therefore need to be familiar with the cultural background!

60 saaTh

6 Travel in India and Pakistan

Key expressions

māĩ Tren sTeshan jaanaa chaahtii hūũ	I want to go to the railway station (fem.)
māĩ Tren sTeshan jaanaa chaahtaa hūũ	I want to go to the railway station (masc.)
mujhe dihlii kii ek vaapasii TikaT chaahiiye	I would like one return ticket to Delhi.
mujhe laahaur kii do vaapasii TikaT chaahiiyē	I would like two return tickets to Lahore.
kitne paise?	How much money?
kul . . . . . rupaie	Altogether . . . . . rupees.
kaunsii bas dihlii jaatii-hai?	Which bus goes to Delhi?
laahaur jaane-vaalii bas kaunsii hai?	Which is the Lahore − going bus? i.e. Which is the bus for Lahore?

Conversations

1 Helen wants to go to the railway station. She gets into a taxi and asks how much it will cost

HELEN māĩ Tren sTeshan jaanaa chaahtii hūũ.[1] kitne paise?

TAXI DRIVER tiis rupaie.

HELEN Thiik hai.

TAXI DRIVER baiThiiye.[2]

2 Helen is buying a train ticket for Lahore at the station

HELEN   mujhe laahaur kii do vaapasii TikaT
          chaahiiye[3] – ek mere liiye aur ek merii
          beTii ke liiye.
          kitne paise?
CLERK   aap ke liiye chaaliis rupaie aur aap kii beTii
          ke liiye biis rupaie. kul saaTh rupaie.
HELEN   liijiiye[4] saaTh rupaie.
CLERK   TikaT liijiiye.

3 Peter is in New Delhi at a bus stop trying to get a bus to Old Delhi and asks a passer-by

PETER   muaaf kiijiiye, saahib.[5]
            puuranii dihlii jaane-vaalii bas kaunsii[6]
            hai?
PASSER-BY   bas nambar pachchiis hai.
PETER   aur bas nambar pachchiis yahãã se[7]
            jaatii hai?
PASSER-BY   jii hãã.
PETER   achchhaa, shukriiyaa.

4 A bus arrives (but not a 25) and Peter asks the driver

PETER   kyaa, ye bas puraanii dihlii jaatii hai?
DRIVER   jii nahĩĩ.
PETER   kaunsii bas puraanii dihlii jaatii hai?
DRIVER   bas nambar pachchiis liijiye.
          aur bas nambar pãĩtiis bhii puraanii dihlii
          jaatii hai.
PETER   achchhaa, shukriiyaa.

Explanations

1 *mai . . . . . jaanaa chaahtii hũũ/chaahtaa hũũ*
jaanaa means 'to go', and *chaahnaa* 'to want'.

2 *baiThiiye*
'Please sit down'

3 *mujhe . . . . chaahiiye*
Literally 'to me . . . is required' i.e. 'I need . . . .'
chaahiiye agrees with its object in number; the
plural form is simply nasalised, for example:

mujhe ek TikaT chaahiiye	I need one ticket
mujhe do TikaT chaahiiyẽ	I need two tickets
mujhe rikshaa nahĩ̃ chaahiiye	I don't need a rickshaw
mujhe taiksii nahĩ̃ chaahiiye	I don't need a taxi

4 *liijiiye*
'Please take', is the polite form of the command
from the verb *lenaa*, 'to take'.

5 *muaaf kiijiiye, saahib*
This means 'Excuse me, sir' (literally 'Please do
my forgiveness').

6 *kaunsii?/kaunsaa?*
This means 'which?' For example:

ye kaunsaa hoTal hai?	Which hotel is this?
kaunsii Tren/bas . . . jaatii hai?	Which train/bus goes to . . .?
laahaur jaane-vaalii bas kaunsii hai?	Which is the bus for Lahore? ('Which is the Lahore-going bus?')

7 *yahãã se*
This means 'from here' (literally 'here from').

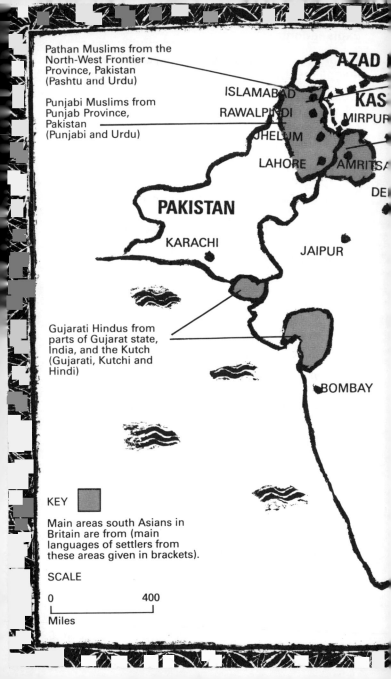

Pathan Muslims from the
North-West Frontier
Province, Pakistan
(Pashtu and Urdu)

Punjabi Muslims from
Punjab Province,
Pakistan
(Punjabi and Urdu)

AZAD

ISLAMABAD
RAWALPINDI
KAS
MIRPUR
JHELUM
LAHORE
AMRITSA
DE

PAKISTAN

KARACHI
JAIPUR

Gujarati Hindus from
parts of Gujarat state,
India, and the Kutch
(Gujarati, Kutchi and
Hindi)

BOMBAY

KEY

Main areas south Asians in
Britain are from (main
languages of settlers from
these areas given in brackets).

SCALE

0   400

Miles

KASHMIR

Punjabi Muslims from the Mirpur border with Kashmir (Punjabi and Urdu)

Punjabi Sikhs from Punjab state, India (Punjabi and Hindi)

Sylheti Bengali Muslims from the Bangladesh border with Assam (Sylheti dialect of Bengali)

AGRA

LUCKNOW

VARANASI

INDIA

BANGLA –DESH

CALCUTTA

ASSAM

BURMA

Bengali Muslims (Bengali)

SRI LANKA

INDIA AND PAKISTAN

. kahãã hai?	Where is . . .?
laahaur jaane-vaalii Tren kahãã se jaatii hai?	Where does the train to Lahore go from?
kyaa, ye laahaur jaane-vaalii Tren hai?	Is this the train for Lahore?
kyaa, ye Tren laahaur jaatii hai?	Does this train go to Lahore?
baazaar	market, bazaar
safar kitne ghanTe ka hai?	How many hours is the journey?
ek ghanTaa	one hour
do (tiin, chaar . . .)	two (three, four . . .)
ghanTe	hours
ek din	one day
do din	two days
aaj	today

Exercises

1 You are a woman visiting Delhi. Tell a taxi driver that you want to go to:
(a)   the railway station
(b)   a hotel
(c)   jamaa masjid (the great mosque of Old Delhi)

2 You are a man visiting Delhi. Tell a taxi driver that you want to go to:
(a)   laal qilaa (Lal Qila: the Red Fort, Delhi)
(b)   the market
(c)   puraanii dihlii (Old Delhi)

3 Say you need/want:
(a)   a taxi
(b)   a rickshaw
(c)   the bus for Old Delhi
(d)   a ticket
(e)   two tickets to Lahore
(f)   a return ticket to Jhelum

4 Say in Hindi/Urdu
(a)   Where is the bus stop?
(b)   How much money?
(c)   Which bus goes to the railway station?
(d)   Bus number 4
(e)   Where does the bus to the railway station go from?
(f)   Where does bus number 4 go from?

5 Take the passenger's part in this conversation at the railway station.
YOU	(Hello, I want a return ticket to Jaipur)
CLERK	achchhaa. Jaipur kii ek vaapasii TikaT.
YOU	(How much?)
CLERK	tiis rupaie.
YOU	(Here are 30 rupees.)

Worth knowing

Trains are best for long journeys in India and Pakistan unless you can afford to travel by plane. You can travel by train 1st class air-conditioned or not air-conditioned, 2nd class reserved or unreserved, or 3rd class. 2nd class unreserved can get very crowded. It is a good idea to reserve your seats and to reserve sleepers, 1st or 2nd class, especially before a long journey, several days beforehand. This will save you hours of queueing.

Railway station restaurants are generally good, and at almost every station there are vendors of snacks – samosas, bananas or other fruit in season. They sell their wares from the platform through the train windows or come on to the train while it stops. They also sell hot tea, served in 'disposable' clay cups, thrown out of the window when the train moves on. Apart from railway stations, there are many good cheap restaurants. However, unless you are eating in a private home, it is sensible to choose well-cooked food and drink boiled water – tea is always available – or bottled drinks. In India, even food in five-star hotels is very cheap by western standards, so you can treat yourself occasionally!

Within the cities, buses are an excellent way of getting about, being fast, frequent and cheap, but they can be terribly overcrowded, so be prepared to stand. More expensive are taxis and rickshaws, which are rather like motor scooters designed to carry two passengers and a driver. Some are metered; otherwise be prepared to bargain. A more leisurely way of getting about is by tonga, a horse-drawn two-wheeler, and it is often also possible to hire bicycles.

Take as little clothing as possible, as clothes are easily and cheaply bought in India and Pakistan,

either ready-made or made to measure by a ta[...]
In any case they are often more appropriate for
the climate! It is advisable to dress modestly by
covering arms and legs. This applies especially to
women travellers in Pakistan but perhaps less so
in India, where people are more used to tourists
and travellers.

70 sattar

Can you get by?

Try this exercise when you have finished this course, and check your answers on p. 84-5. You might like to note your mistakes and then try the exercise again to see if you have improved.

Socialising
1. Greet a Muslim
2. Greet a Hindu
3. Reply to 'assalaam alaikum'
4. Greet a Sikh
5. Ask 'How are you?'
6. Say 'I'm fine, thanks!'
7. Say 'Goodbye' to a Muslim
8. Say 'My name is Anna Martin'
9. Ask 'What is your full name?'
10. Ask 'Is your full name Paramjeet Singh?'

Family
11. Ask 'Are you married?'
12. Ask 'Do you have children?'
13. Ask 'How many children do you have?
14. Say 'I have five children'
15. Say 'I have two daughters'
16. Say 'I have one son'
17. Ask 'Who is this?' (about someone junior)
18. Ask 'Who is this?' (about someone senior)
19. Say 'This is my son'
20. Say 'These are my children'

Work and home
21. Say you're a teacher
22. Ask a man what work he does
23. Ask a woman what work she does
24. Ask a woman where she works
25. Ask a man where he works
26. Say you work in a hospital (you're a woman)
27. Say you work in Bradford (you're a man)

28 Say you live in Rochdale (you're a woman)
29 Say you live in Glasgow (you're a man)
30 Ask a man where he lives
31 Ask a woman where she lives
32 Ask 'What's your telephone number?'
33 Ask 'What's your address'?

Health
34 Ask a man how he is
35 Ask a woman how she is
36 Say 'I'm not well'
37 Ask 'What's the matter?'
38 Ask 'Where's the pain?'
39 Say 'Please show me'
40 Say 'I have a fever'
41 Say 'I have a cough'
42 Say 'I have a cold'
43 Say 'I have a headache'
44 Say 'I have stomach ache'
45 Say 'Don't worry'

Travel
46 Ask for a return ticket to Lahore
47 Ask for two tickets to Delhi
48 Say 'I want to go to the station' (you're a woman)
49 Say 'I want to go to the bus stop' (you're a man)
50 Ask 'Is this the bus for Jaipur?'
51 Say 'I need a taxi'
52 Ask 'How much (money)?'
53 Ask 'Where is the bus stop?'
54 Ask 'Where does the bus for Delhi go from?'
55 Ask 'Which is the bus for Lahore?'

Appendix

Useful phrases

phir kahiiye	Please say it again
zaraa aahistaa boliiye	Please speak slowly
mãi nahĩ samjhaa	I (male) don't understand
mãi nahĩ samjhii	I (female) don't understand
mujhe maaluum nahĩ	I don't know
mujhe yaad nahĩ	I don't remember
'shoe' ko hindii/urduu mẽ kyaa kahte hãi?	What do you call 'shoe' in Hindi/Urdu?
'bhaaii' ke maanii kyaa hãi?	What does *bhaaii* mean?
aapko angrezii atii hai?	Do you speak English?

Numbers

These are written in Devanagari and Arabic scripts and in the western way: Hindi/Urdu speakers are generally familiar with both Devanagari or Arabic and western numerals. Here are the numbers from 0 - 100, and at intervals up to 1 million.

0	*syfar*	39	*untaaliis*
1	*ek*	40	*chaaliis*
2	*do*	41	*iktaaliis*
3	*tiin*	42	*beaaliis*
4	*chaar*	43	*tāītaaliis*
5	*pāāch*	44	*cavaaliis*
6	*chhai*	45	*pāītaaliis*
7	*saat*	46	*chhiaaliis*
8	*aaTh*	47	*sāītaaliis*
9	*nau*	48	*aRtaaliis*
10	*das*	49	*unanchaas*
11	*giaaraa*	50	*pachaas*
12	*baaraa*	51	*ikiaavan*
13	*teraa*	52	*baavan*
14	*caudaa*	53	*trepan*
15	*pandraa*	54	*cavvan*
16	*solaa*	55	*pachpan*
17	*satraa*	56	*chhappan*
18	*aTThaaraa*	57	*sattaavan*
19	*unniis*	58	*aTThaavan*
20	*biis*	59	*unsaTh*
21	*ikkis*	60	*saaTh*
22	*baaiis*	61	*iksaTh*
23	*taiis*	62	*baasaTh*
24	*caubiis*	63	*tresaTh*
25	*pachchiis*	64	*chāusaTh*
26	*chhabbiis*	65	*pāisaTh*
27	*sattaaiis*	66	*chhiaasaTh*
28	*aTThaaiis*	67	*sarsaTh*
29	*unattiis*	68	*aRsaTh*
30	*tiis*	69	*unhattar*
31	*ikattiis*	70	*sattar*
32	*battiis*	71	*ikhattar*
33	*tāītiis*	72	*bahattar*
34	*cāutiis*	73	*tihattar*
35	*pāītiis*	74	*chauhattar*
36	*chhattiis*	75	*pichhattar*
37	*sāītiis*	76	*chihattar*
38	*aRtiis*	77	*sathattar*

78	aThattar	90	navve
79	unaasii	91	ikiaanave
80	assii	92	baanve
81	ikiaasii	93	triaanve
82	beaasii	94	chauraanve
83	tiraasii	95	pachaanve
84	chauraasii	96	chhiaanve
85	pachaasii	97	sattaanve
86	chhiaasii	98	aTThaanve
87	sataasii	99	ninaanave
88	aThaasii	100	sau
89	navaasii		

200	do sau	300	tiin sau (and so on)

1000 *ek hazaar*
2000 *do hazaar* (and so on)
100 000 *ek laakh*
200 000 *do laakh* (and so on)
1000 000 *das laakh*

Days of the week

These are called by different names depending on the religious and cultural background of the speaker:

	Hindi	*Urdu*
Sunday	*itvaar/raviivaar*	*itvaar*
Monday	*somvaar*	*piir/somvaar*
Tuesday	*mangalvaar*	*mangal*
Wednesday	*budhvaar*	*budh*
Thursday	*brihaspatiivaar, guruuvaar*	*jumeraat*
Friday	*shukravaar*	*jumaa*
Saturday	*shaniivaar*	*saniichar/haftaa*

Further study

For information on course books and courses available in Britain for learning Hindi and Urdu, contact The Centre for Information on Language Teaching (C.I.L.T.), Regent's College, Inner Circle, Regent's Park, London NW1. Tel: 01-486 8221.

Answers to exercises

Unit 1

1 (a) Sikh
   (b) Hindu
   (c) Muslim

2 (a) salaam alaikum
   (b) halo
   (c) namaste
   (d) sat srii akaal

3 (a) halo, aapkaa kyaa haal hai?
   (b) shukriiyaa, mãi Thiik hũũ.

4 (a) RAJ   halo aabid, aapkaa kyaa haal hai?
       ABID   shukriiyaa, mãi Thiik hũũ.
   (b) ABID   aur aapkaa kyaa haal hai?
       RAJ   mãi Thiik hũũ, shukriiyaa.

5 (a) assalaam alaikum   vaalaikum salaam
   (b) aapkaa kyaa haal hai?   shukriiyaa, mãi
                              Thiik hũũ.

Unit 2

1 (a) meraa naam . . . . hai.
   (b) meraa puuraa naam . . . . hai.

2 (a) aapkaa naam kyaa hai?
   (b) aapkaa puuraa naam kyaa hai?
   (c) aapkaa naam aziiz hai?

3 (a) RAJ   halo, aapkaa naam kyaa hai?
       ABID   meraa naam aabid hai.
   (b) SUE   aapkaa naam parviin hai?
       PARVEEN   jii hãa, meraa naam parviin
                 hai.

4 (a) aapkaa naam kyaa hai?
(b) meraa naam Helen hai.
(c) aapkaa puuraa naam Helen Allen hai?
(d) jii hā̄a, meraa puuraa naam Helen Allen hai.
(e) jii nahī̄, meraa naam rajiiv nahī̄ hai, meraa naam raaj hai.

Unit 3
1 (a) aap shaadii-shudaa hā̄ı?
(b) aapke bachche hā̄ı?
(c) aapke kitne bachche hā̄ı?
(d) aapkii kitnii beTiiyā̄a hā̄ı?
(e) aapke kitne beTe hā̄ı?

2 (a) jii hā̄a, mā̄ı shaadii-shudaa hū̄u.
(b) jii hā̄a, mere bachche hā̄ı.
(c) mere chaar bachche hā̄ı.
(d) merii do beTiiyā̄a hā̄ı.
(e) mere do beTe hā̄ı.

3 (a) jii hā̄a, mā̄ı shaadii-shudaa hū̄u.
(b) jii hā̄a, mere bachche hā̄ı.
(c) mere chhai bachche hā̄ı.
(d) merii ek beTii hai.
(e) mere pā̄ach beTe hā̄ı.

4 (a) jii hā̄a, mā̄ı shaadii-shudaa hū̄u.
(b) jii hā̄a, mere bachche hā̄ı.
(c) mere chaar bachche hā̄ı.
(d) merii tiin beTiiyā̄a hā̄ı.
(e) meraa ek beTaa hai.

5 (a) aap shaadii-shudaa hā̄ı?
(b) aapke bachche hā̄ı?
(c) ye kaun hā̄ı?
(d) aapke kitne bachche hā̄ı?
(e) aapkaa ek beTaa hai?
(f) aapkii ek beTii hai?

Unit 4

1 (a) meraa naam kamiljiit kaur hai.
   (b) mãi soshal varkar hũu.

2 (a) meraa naam Peter Harris hai.
   (b) mãi akaunTanT hũu.

3 aapkaa naam kyaa hai?
   aap kyaa kaam kartii hãi?

4 aapkaa naam kyaa hai?
   aap kyaa kaam karte hãi?

5 JUNE Ann, aap DaakTar hãi?
   ANN jii nahĩĩ, mãi DaakTar nahĩĩ hũu. mãi akaunTanT hũu.

6 (a) nasiim, aap kahãã rahte hãi?
      mãi Coventry mẽ rahtaa hũu.
   (b) ushaa, aap kahãã rahtii hãi?
      mãi Birmingham mẽ rahtii hũu.
   (c) 'amiinaa, aap kahãã rahtii hãi?
      mãi Glasgow mẽ rahtii hũu.
   (d) amritaa, aap kahãã rahtii hãi?
      mãi London mẽ rahtii hũu.
   (e) raaj, aap kahãã rahte hãi?
      mãi Delhi mẽ rahtaa hũu.
   (f) Jenny, aap kahãã rahtii hãi?
      mãi Manchester mẽ rahtii hũu.
   (g) amrit, aap kahãã rahte hãi?
      mãi Walsall mẽ rahtaa hũu.
   (h) Bob, aap kahãã rahte hãi?
      mãi Derby mẽ rahtaa hũu.

7 (a) aapkaa puuraa naam kyaa hai?
   (b) aap kahãã rahtii hãi?
   (*or:* aapkaa pataa kyaa hai?)
   (c) aapkaa Teliifon nambar kyaa hai?
   (d) aap kyaa kaam kartii hãi?

Unit 5

1   (a) aap kaisii hãĩ? (*or:* aapkaa kyaa haal hai?)
    (b) aap kaise hãĩ? (*or:* aapkaa kyaa haal hai?)
    (c) kyaa baat hai?
    (d) dard kahãã hai?

2   (a) mujhe buKhaar hai.
    (b) mujhe khaansii hai.
    (c) mujhe zukaam hai.
    (d) mujhe dard hai.

3   (a) dard peT mẽ hai.
    (b) dard sar mẽ hai.
    (c) dard ũgliiyõ mẽ hai.
    (d) dard Tããg mẽ hai.
    (e) dard hath mẽ hai.
    (f) dard sĩine mẽ hai.
    (g) dard paaõ mẽ hai.
    (h) dard ããkhõ mẽ hai.

4   HEALTH VISITOR   aap kaisii hãĩ?
    SHAMIM BEGUM   mãĩ Thiik nahĩĩ hũũ.
    HEALTH VISITOR   kyaa baat hai?
    SHAMIM BEGUM   mere peT mẽ dard hai.

5   (a) mujhe haath dikhaaiiye.
    (b) mujhe naak dikhaaiiye.
    (c) mujhe galaa dikhaaiiye.
    (d) mujhe ũgliiỹãã dikhaaiiye.
    (e) mujhe Tããg dikhaaiiye.
    (f) mujhe baah dikhaaiiye.
    (g) mujhe donõ baahẽ dikhaaiiye.
    (h) mujhe paaõ dikhaaiiye.

Unit 6

1. (a) mãi Tren sTeshan jaanaa chaahtii hũũ.
   (b) mãi hoTal jaanaa chaahtii hũũ.
   (c) mãi jamaa masjid jaanaa chaahtii hũũ.

2. (a) mãi laal qilaa jaanaa chaahtaa hũũ.
   (b) mãi baazaar jaanaa chaahtaa hũũ.
   (c) mãi puraanii dihlii jaanaa chaahtaa hũũ.

3. (a) mujhe taiksii chaahiiye.
   (b) mujhe rikshaa chaahiiye.
   (c) mujhe puraanii dihlii jaane-vaalii bas
       chaahiiye.
   (d) mujhe TikaT chaahiiye.
   (e) mujhe laahaur kii do TikaT chaahiiyẽ.
   (f) mujhe jhelum kii ek vaapasii TikaT
       chaahiiye.

4. (a) bas sTaap kahãã hai?
   (b) kitne paise?
   (c) kaunsii bas Tren sTeshan jaatii hai?
   (d) bas nambar chaar.
   (e) Tren sTeshan jaane-vaalii bas kahãã se
       jaatii hai?
   (f) chaar nambar bas kahãã se jaatii hai?

5. (a) halo, mujhe jaaiipuur kii ek vaapasii TikaT
       chaahiiye.
   (b) kitne paise?
   (c) liijiiye tiis rupaie.

Answers to 'Can you get by?'
Socialising
1 assalaam alaikum
2 namaste
3 vaalaikum salaam
4 sat srii akaal
5 aapkaa kyaa haal hai?
 (*or* aap kaisii hãi? (to a woman)/aap kaise hãi?
 (to a man)
6 mãi Thiik hũu, shukriiyaa
7 Khudaa haafiz
8 meraa naam Anna Martin hai
9 aapkaa puuraa naam kyaa hai?
10 aapkaa puuraa naam paramjiit singh hai?

Family
11 aap shaadii-shudaa hãi?
12 aapke bachche hãi?
13 aapke kitne bachche hãi?
14 mere pãach bachche hãi
15 merii do beTiiyãa hãi
16 meraa ek beTaa hai
17 ye kaun hai?
18 ye kaun hãi?
19 ye meraa beTaa hai
20 ye mere bachche hãi

Work and home
21 mãi Tiichar hũu
22 aap kyaa kaam karte hãi?
23 aap kyaa kaam kartii hãi?
24 aap kahãa kaam kartii hãi?
25 aap kahãa kaam karte hãi?
26 mãi haspiTaal mẽ kaam kartii hũu
27 mãi Bradford mẽ kaam kartaa hũu
28 mãi Rochdale mẽ rahtii hũu
29 mãi Glasgow mẽ rahtaa hũu
30 aap kahãa rahte hãi?
31 aap kahãa rahtii hãi?
32 aapkaa Teliifon nambar kyaa hai?
33 aapkaa pataa kyaa hai?

Health

34 aap kaise hãĩ?
35 aap kaisii hãĩ?
36 mãĩ Thiik nahĩĩ hũu
37 kyaa baat hai?
38 dard kahãã hai?
39 mujhe dikhaaiiye
40 mujhe buKhaar hai
41 mujhe khaansii hai
42 mujhe zukaam hai
43 mere sar mẽ dard hai
44 mere peT mẽ dard hai
45 fikr naa kiijiiye

Travel

46 mujhe laahaur kii ek vaapasii TikaT chaahiiye
47 mujhe dihlii kii do TikaT chaahiiyẽ
48 mãĩ sTeshan jaanaa chaatii hũu
49 mãĩ bas sTaap jaanaa chaahtaa hũu
50 ye jaaiipuur jaane-vaalii bas hai? *or* ye bas jaaiipuur jaatii hai?
51 mujhe taiksii chaahiiye
52 kitne paise?
53 bas sTaap kahãã hai?
54 dilhii jaane-vaalii bas kahãã se jaatii hai?
55 kaunsii bas lahaur jaatii hai? *or* lahaur jaane-vaalii bas kaunsii hai?

Word lists

The numbers and other words which appear in the appendix are not listed here.

Hindi/Urdu – English

a aaiiye — please come
aaj — today
āākh — eye
aanaa — to come
aap — you
aapkaa/kii/ke — your
ab — now
achchhaa — right!, really! I see
achchhaa/ii — good
aglaa/ii/e — (the) next
aur — and

b baah — arm
baap — father
baat — thing, matter
baazaar — bazaar, market
bachchaa — (male) child
bachche — children
bachchii — (female) child
bahan — sister
bahut — a lot, very
baiThiiye — please sit down
baiThnaa — to sit down
baRaa/ii/e — big, large, elder
bas sTaap — bus stop
berozgaar — unemployed
beTaa — son
beTii — daughter
bhaaii — brother
bhii — also
biimaar — ill
biivii (Urdu) — wife
buKhaar — fever, temperature

c	*chaae*	tea
	chaahiiye	is needed/required
	chaahiiyē	are needed/required
	chaahnaa	to want
	chhoTaa/ii/e	small, younger

d	*daadaa*	grandfather (paternal)
	daadii	grandmother (paternal)
	dard	pain
	davaaii	medicine
	dikhaaiiye	please show
	dikhaanaa	to show
	din	day
	dopahr	midday
	dukaan	shop
	DaakTar	doctor

| f | *fikr* | worry |

g	*galaa*	throat
	garmii	heat, warmth
	ghanTaa	hour
	ghar	home
	golii	tablet
	guDbaaii	goodbye
	guTnaa	knee

h	*haal*	health, state
	haath	hand
	haftaa	week
	hai	is
	hāi	are, is (courteous)
	halo	hello
	haspiTaal	hospital
	helth vizitar	health visitor

j	*jaaiiye*	please go
	jaanaa	to go
	jii hāā	yes
	jii nahī̃	no

k		
	kaam	work
	kaam karnaa	to work
	kaan	ear
	kahãã?	where?
	karnaa	to do
	kaun?	who?
	kaunsaa/ii/e	which?
	. . . ke baad	after . . .
	khaaiiye	to eat
	khaanaa	please eat
	khaanaa	food
	khaansii	cough
	khaRe hojaaiiye	please stand up
	kitnaa/ii/e	how many?/how much?
	kuchh	some
l	*laRkaa*	boy
	laRkii	girl
	leTiiye	please lie down
	leTnaa	to lie down
	liijiiye	please take
m	*mãã*	mother
	mahiinaa	month
	mãĩ	I
	mẽ	in
	meraa/ii/e	my
	miDvaaif	midwife
n	*naak*	nose
	naam	name
	naanaa	grandfather (maternal)
	naanii	grandmother (maternal)
	nambar	number
p	*paanii*	water
	paaõ	foot
	pahũchnaa	to arrive
	paise	money

	pataa	address
	patii (Hindi)	husband
	patnii (Hindi)	wife
	peT	stomach
	puuraa	full
r	raat	night
	rahnaa	to live
	rozaanaa	everyday
	rupaiaa	rupee
s	saal	year
	saas	mother-in-law
	safar	journey
	sar	head
	sardii	cold
	se	from
	se pahle	before
	siinaa	chest
	sojan	swelling
	soshal varkar	social worker
	subah	morning
	susar	father-in-law
sh	shaadii-shudaa	married
	shaam	evening
	shauhar (Urdu)	husband
	shukriiyaa	thank you
t	tiisre pahr	afternoon
	Tāāg	leg
	Teliifon	telephone
	Thiik	all right, fine, OK
	Tiichar	teacher
	Tikat	ticket
	Tren	train
v	vaapasii	return
u	ūglii	finger

y	yahāā	here
	ye	she, he, they, it, this, these
z	zukaam	a cold

English – Hindi/Urdu

A
address	*pataa*
after . . .	*. . . ke baad*
afternoon	*tiisre pahr*
all right, fine, OK	*Thiik*
also	*bhii*
and	*aur*
are, is (courteous)	*hāĩ*
arm	*baah*
to arrive	*pahũchnaa*

B
bazaar	*baazaar*
before	*se pahle*
big	*baRaa/ii/e*
boy	*laRkaa*
brother	*bhaaii*
bus stop	*bas sTaap*

C
chest	*siinaa*
child (female)	*bachchii*
child (male)	*bachchaa*
children	*bachche*
cold	*sardii*
a cold	*zukaam*
to come	*aanaa*
(please) come	*aaiiye*
cough	*khaansii*

D
daughter	*beTii*
day	*din*
to do	*karnaa*
doctor	*DaakTar*

E
ear	*kaan*
to eat	*khaanaa*
(please) eat	*khaaiiye*
elder	*baRaa/baRii*
evening	*shaam*
everyday	*rozaanaa*
eye	*āākh*

F	father	*baap*
	father-in-law	*susar*
	fever	*buKhaar*
	fine, OK	*Thiik*
	finger	*ūglii*
	food	*khaanaa*
	foot	*paaõ*
	from	*se*
	full (name)	*puuraa (naam)*

G	girl	*laRkii*
	to go	*jaanaa*
	(please) go	*jaaiiye*
	good	*achchhaa/ii*
	goodbye	*guDbaaii*
		Khudaa haafiz (Muslims)
	grandfather (maternal)	*naanaa*
	grandfather (paternal)	*daadaa*
	grandmother (maternal)	*naanii*
	grandmother (paternal)	*daadii*

H	hand	*haath*
	he	*ye*
	head	*sar*
	health, state	*haal*
	health visitor	*helth vizitar*
	heat, warmth	*garmii*
	hello	*halo*
	here	*yahāã*
	home	*ghar*
	hospital	*haspiTaal*
	hour	*ghanTaa*
	how many?	*kitnaa/ii/e*
	husband	*patii (Hindi)*
		shauhar (Urdu)

I	I	*mãi*
	ill	*biimaar*
	in	*mē*
	is	*hai (courteously: hãi)*
	it	*ye*
J	journey	*safar*
K	knee	*guTnaa*
L	large	*baRaa/ii/e*
	leg	*Tãag*
	to lie down	*leTnaa*
	(please) lie down	*leTiiye*
	to live	*rahnaa*
	(a) lot	*bahut*
M	market	*baazaar*
	married	*shaadii-shudaa*
	matter	*baat*
	medicine	*davaaii*
	midday	*dopahr*
	midwife	*miDvaaif*
	money	*paise*
	month	*mahiinaa*
	morning	*subah*
	mother	*mãa*
	mother-in-law	*saas*
	my	*meraa/ii/e*
N	name	*naam*
	is needed/required	*chaahiiye*
	are needed/required	*chaahiiyē*
	next	*aglaa/ii/e*
	night	*raat*
	no	*jii nahĩ*
	nose	*naak*
	now	*ab*
	number	*nambar*
P	pain	*dard*

R	really!	*achchhaa!*
	return ticket	*vaapasii TikaT*
	right!	*achchhaa!*
	rupee	*rupaiaa*

S	she	*ye*
	shop	*dukaan*
	to show	*dikhaanaa*
	(please) show	*dikhaaiiye*
	sister	*bahan*
	to sit down	*baiThnaa*
	(please) sit down	*baiThiiye*
	small, younger	*chhoTaa/ii/e*
	social worker	*soshal varkar*
	some	*kuchh*
	son	*beTaa*
	(please) stand up	*khaRe hojaaiiye*
	stomach	*peT*
	swelling	*sojan*

T	tablet	*golii*
	(please) take	*liijiiye*
	tea	*chaae*
	teacher	*Tiichar*
	telephone	*Teliifon*
	temperature/fever	*buKhaar*
	thank you	*shukriiyaa*
	these	*ye*
	they	*ye*
	thing	*baat*
	this	*ye*
	throat	*galaa*
	ticket	*TikaT*
	today	*aaj*
	train	*Tren*

U	unemployed	*berozgaar*

V	very	*bahut*

W want	*chaahnaa*
water	*paanii*
week	*haftaa*
where	*kahãã*
which	*kaunsaa/ii/e*
who	*kaun*
wife	*patnii* (Hindi)
	biivii (Urdu)
work	*kaam*
to work	*kaam karnaa*
worry	*fikr*
Y year	*saal*
yes	*jii hãã*
you	*aap*
younger	*chhoTaa/chhoTii*
your	*aapkaa/kii/ke*